MARILYN, NORMA JEAN AND ME

A dramatization of the movie star's secret plan to leave Hollywood for Broadway

MARILYN, NORMA JEAN AND ME

A dramatization of the movie star's secret plan to leave Hollywood for Broadway

J. Ajlouny

MARILYN, NORMA JEAN AND ME

A dramatization of the movie star's secret plan to leave Hollywood for Broadway

Copyright © 2018, 1998
by J. Ajlouny
All rights reserved

Push Pull Press
An Imprint of:
Fresh Ink Group, LLC
Box 931
Guntersville, AL 35976
Email: info@FreshInkGroup.com
FreshInkGroup.com

Edition 1.0   1998
Edition 2.0   2018

Cover art by Anik
Cover by Stephen Geez

Performance: Any performance of this play must be licensed in writing by the publisher, including royalty arrangements. No alterations, deletions, or substitutions of a material nature may be made in this work without prior written permission of Fresh Ink Group, LLC. Authorship credit must appear on all programs and promotions in all media where space permits.

Publication: Except as permitted under the U.S. Copyright Act of 1976, no part of this publication may be reproduced, distributed, or transmitted in any form or by any means, or stored in a database or retrieval system, without prior written permission of Fresh Ink Group, LLC.

BISAC Subject Headings:
PER013000   PERFORMING ARTS / Theater / Broadway & Musicals
PER011000   PERFORMING ARTS / Theater / General
DRA001000   DRAMA / American / General

Library of Congress Control Number: 2018930316

ISBN-13: 978-1-936442-77-5 Softcover
ISBN-13: 978-1-936442-81-2 Hardcover
ISBN-13: 978-1-936442-78-2 Ebooks

Marilyn, Norma Jean and Me

A dramatization of the movie star's
secret plan to leave Hollywood for Broadway

J. Ajlouny

Time: Spring and Summer 1962

Place: New York City

Setting: The office/studio of musical director Jerry Ross. It is messy and obvious he frequently sleeps there too. Its most prominent feature is a piano.

Characters:

Marilyn Monroe: as herself, age 35

Jerry Ross: a middle-aged pianist and composer who is devoted to his music and to musical theater. He is friendly, reticent, kind, blunt, curious and impatient.

Summary:

In the months prior to her untimely death in August 1962, Marilyn Monroe seeks out the services of a musical director to help her develop a one-person theatrical show about her life and her struggles coping with worldwide fame. The play includes two performances by her, "Diamonds Are A Girl's Best Friend" and "I Wanna Be Loved By You." It closes with an original song performed soulfully by Jerry Ross, "Growing New You."

Act I

Jerry Ross is standing above his piano, obviously bored. He pounds out a series of sharp notes with his index finger. He repeats the pattern. As he begins again, he hears a faint knocking at the door. He looks up and listens closely. Hearing nothing, he repeats the pattern. In silence, he once again believes he hears a faint knock. He walks slowly toward the door. Again, a faint knocking is heard.

Jerry Ross:
(Shouting) It's open!

Marilyn Monroe:
(Voice) It's stuck!

Jerry:
Just kick the damn thing!

He rushes back to the piano and sits down to make it look like he is hard at work. Suddenly, Marilyn Monroe stumbles in, having mastered the door less than gracefully. She is wearing a black wig, hat and overcoat.

Marilyn:
(Slightly embarrassed) Oh.

She straightens herself.

Jerry:
(His back still turned) I'll be right with you.

Marilyn:
Sure, take your time. I doubt you're expecting me.

Upon hearing Marilyn's distinctive voice, he straightens his back with a sudden start. He raises his finger in thought, then shakes his head.

Jerry:
(To himself) Naaaw, it can't be. (He picks up a hand mirror from the top of his piano and raises it up to spot her reflection. He peers into it. Stage lights darken. A single spotlight shines on Marilyn, who is still. Lights go up.) I knew it couldn't be. I ain't that lucky!

He brushes aside the thought and resumes his work. Marilyn looks around, stepping softly, careful not to disturb him. She sheds her hat and coat, revealing a simple dress. She shakes out her hair and straightens herself out, make believing the audience is a full length mirror. She slowly walks toward him while his back is still turned.

Marilyn:
I'm sorry I showed up without an appointment. But if I did have an appointment, I

probably would have been late anyway. So that's why I don't like to make appointments anymore.

Jerry again raises his back and partially turns his head in apprehension. Marilyn, turns around and slowly walks back to the table upon which she has laid her coat. Jerry again raises the mirror to peer at her. Marilyn bends forward to pick up a magazine from the floor. At this exact moment, again the stage lights go dark and a single spotlight captures Marilyn in a sexy, slow motion movement. Lights go up. Jerry shakes his head in disbelief. He raises the mirror for a second look. Again, lights go dark except for the spotlight on Marilyn. This time Marilyn turns around and looks straight at him. Lights go up.

Jerry:

It is! (He jumps up, turns around and extends his hand in greeting as he walks toward her.) Who needs appointments nowadays except at the dentist's office. Hello, I'm Gerald Ross, but everyone calls me Jerry. Welcome to my parlor.

Marilyn:

Thank you very much. I hope I'm not interrupting anything.

Jerry:
Well, if boredom is something to interrupt, then I guess you are.

Marilyn:
Will you please forgive me? I can come back, if you like. I'm not sure exactly when, though. (She looks perplexed)

Jerry:
Not at all. Please, make yourself comfortable. Can I get you anything?

Marilyn:
No, thank you I'm fine. I just wanted to meet you. Dean told me I should meet you.

Jerry:
Dean?

Marilyn:
Yes, Dean Martin. He told me you arranged some songs for him a couple of years ago.

Jerry:
Yes I did. Funny, I never thought he liked me much, not after I told him he should get back together with Jerry Lewis.

Marilyn:
No, he spoke very highly of you. He said you personify the musical tradition of the theater better than anybody he knew.

Jerry:
Martin said that?

Marilyn:
Yes. And he said you still owed him $10 for betting on some team or other. So I gave him the money for you. So you owe me ten bucks.

Jerry:
So you came here to collect the money from me?

Marilyn:
No, for goodness sake. But it did give me an excuse to come and see you.

Jerry:
Why in the earth would Marilyn Monroe want to see me?

Marilyn:
That's a fair question.

Jerry:
You know, I don't much care for Hollywood. New York is the place for me.

Marilyn:

I love New York too, especially the theater life here. That's why I'm here, I want to talk to you about helping me produce a show I'd like to bring to the Broadway stage...eventually.

Jerry:

But your a movie actress.

Marilyn:

No, I'm an *actress*, period! It's true most of my work has been in film, but I was once booked to act on stage. But the deal fell through. I figure I've proven myself in the movies. I have two Golden Globes, you know. Now, I want to prove myself in the theater, on the stage. That's real acting; in movies you just have to pretend to act.

Jerry:

I see. You were married to Arthur Miller, an icon of the American theater. How come you didn't do any theater with him?

Marilyn:

Arthur wrote a film for me that started out as a play. It was directed by John Houston, who Arthur always admired. We always wanted to do something for the stage together but it never worked out I guess. Everyone is always so busy thinking about their next movie, and the one after that, that it was difficult to focus on doing a play together. Besides, I think Arthur had some secret qualm against writing a play for me. But when you think about it, I'm not really his type of character, if you know what I mean.

Jerry:
Well, a good actress can play any type of character. That's what I think.

Marilyn:
That's what I think too! But Arthur doesn't feel that way. Obviously. But it would have been wrong for me to ask him to write something for me. He's an *artiste* you know.

Jerry:
And you think I'm not?

Marilyn:
Oh gosh no, Mr. Ross...

Jerry:
Call me Jerry.

Marilyn:
...Jerry. It's just that Dean told me you're a freelance kind of writer. You know, that you can be

hired to work on a show for a salary or something. Arthur doesn't work that way.

Jerry:
I see. So is that why you divorced him, because he wouldn't write a play for you?

Marilyn:
Oh heavens no! We were divorced because we weren't happy together. But we are still good friends. Actually, our relationship has never been better.

Jerry:
Yes, I know what you mean. I get along best with my wife when she's visiting her mother and sisters in Ohio.

Marilyn:
You know what they say about marriage: It's kind of like a hot bath, only it isn't so hot once you get into it.

Jerry:
(Laughing) Funny. You're a funny one.

Marilyn:
Twelve comedies.

Jerry:
Twelve, really? How many movies have you made in all?

Marilyn:
I don't know exactly, somewhere between 25 and 30 of them. The first few I made I was edited out almost entirely. Do they still count?

Jerry:
If you showed up, I think they should.

Marilyn:
Oh, I showed up alright. Back then I would have given my right arm to star in the movies. Now, I'd give my right arm to star in a play.

Jerry:
Be careful what you wish for...

Marilyn:
Oh, I know. But I've given this a lot of thought. I wasn't really prepared for what happened to me in Hollywood. I mean, who can be prepared for stardom? It's something that happens all of a sudden. But it's like quicksand.

Jerry:
Really?

Marilyn:

Yes. But I was so young then. I'm 36 now and I feel I'm ready to tackle other challenges. That's why I've come to see you.

Jerry:

Okay. Sounds fair. What kind of challenges are you speaking about? I'm a musical director, you know, not a psychologist.

Marilyn:

That's funny. I don't know too much about psychology, but I'm learning. I have a psychiatrist in LA. He thinks psychology is poppycock. But I'm not so sure.

Jerry:

Stay here in New York City and work in the theater long enough and you'll be an expert in psychology.

Marilyn:

So I was thinking... Why not produce my own play. I mean, I have my own film production company. Why shouldn't I have my own theatrical production company?

Jerry:

Makes sense, I suppose. But do you have a play to produce?

Marilyn:
No I don't. That's why I've come to see you. You're gonna write one for me.

Jerry:
I don't think you understand, Ms. Monroe. I'm not a ....

Marilyn:
Please call me Marilyn. No. Call me Norma Jean.

Jerry:
Whatever you want. But I'm not a playwright. I compose and direct music for plays. You know, musicals!

Marilyn:
I understand. But certainly you can write a play too? I mean, if you can write music and play the piano, you should be able to write a play too. Gosh, Arthur doesn't play the piano and he writes plays. Besides, I'll help you. It's my story after all, and nobody knows is better than me.

Lights go down over them. Marilyn exits. Light goes up over Jerry.

Jerry:

(To the audience) Thus began my working relationship with Marilyn Monroe. And trust me, I didn't tell a soul. Not even my wife. Who would believe me, anyway? (He turns his piano bench around and sits on it facing the audience.) Marilyn was the best example I've ever seen of that elusive species invariably called "woman-child." I know that sounds belittling, but I don't mean it that way. She was a wonderful person. So innocent, so sweet and so, so natural, if you know what I mean. But she told me at the beginning. "Don't think of me as Marilyn Monroe, think of me as Norma Jean Baker." I'll admit that was pretty hard. But that's the way she wanted it so I did what she told me. Over the next several weeks we met regularly, usually at night. My immediate goal was, of course, to impress her enough to give me the job. Believe me, I need the work. But we never discussed business, not once. I can see how most men could be enthralled by her. I was more intrigued by her than enthralled. I didn't want to possess her; I just wanted to understand her.

Marilyn enters. She is wearing the same hat and coat. Jerry is as before except he is wearing a sweater.

Marilyn:

Sorry I'm late Jerry. The traffic around here tonight is really murder. My driver knows how to maneuver pretty good but there isn't much you can do on a night like this.

She throws off her hat and coat, and looks at the audience again as if it is a mirror.

So where were we?

Jerry:

I'm still interviewing you, remember?

Marilyn:

Okay, shoot.

Jerry:

First of all, tell me, how was your day?

Marilyn:

It was a good day. Nice and quiet. I'm happy to get out of the apartment after dinner. I spent most of the day with my secretary going through mail. You can't believe how much I get. She only shows me the important things, or the really interesting letters. I received sixteen marriage proposals last week. Imagine that?

Jerry:

That doesn't surprise me.

Marilyn:

I mean *only* sixteen! Normally I get at least three dozen a week. I must be slipping.

Jerry:

Impossible. Besides, you remember what you once told me about marriage.

Marilyn:

No, what?

Jerry:

About it being like a hot bath?

Marilyn:

What do you mean?

Jerry:

Never mind, it's not important. (He pulls up two chairs, motions for her sit at the table.)

So tell me, what is your best asset, in your opinion?

Marilyn:

People ask me that all the time. I'd rather you asked me what is my best quality, not asset.

Jerry:

Fair enough. What do you think is your best quality?

Marilyn:

I don't know. People think it's my looks or my body. I prefer to think it's my personality.

Jerry:

I think it's your celebrity. It's the one thing about you which is utterly unique.

Marilyn:

But that's the whole point. I want to get away from the celebrity aspect of my life.

I mean, I know I can't change who I am, but I can change how I am perceived in the future, right?

Jerry:

Have you ever thought about retiring while you're in your prime?

Marilyn:

I don't want to retire. I'm an actress and I care about the craft. That's why I studied at the Actor's Lab in LA and the Actor's Studio here in New York. People sometime think that I must have slept my way to the top. But I never did, nor would I. I wasn't raised like that.

Jerry:

How were you raised then?

Marilyn:

Despite what's been said in the papers, my childhood wasn't that bad. It's true, I didn't have a regular, normal family life, but I was happy...most of the time anyway.

Lights go down, as Marilyn turns to face the audience. Lights over her go up.

My mother is Gladys Monroe, and she had me at a time when things weren't going so well for her. She was married at the time to a man who died before I was born. At birth I was given his name, which was Mortensen, but mom changed it to Baker because that's the name she used. Her first husband was named Jasper Baker, and she had two children by him. But after their divorce he took them to Kentucky without her knowledge, and she couldn't face it. I didn't know this until I was something like 12 years old. By that time, my half-brother Jackie had died and my half-sister Bernice was married with a daughter. Anyway, mom had a tough go of things. You can imagine the difficulty she experienced raising a child on her own. I mean, it's hard now, imagine how it was in the late 1920's and during the Depression.

For this reason, I was sent to live with my grandmother, Della, in the rural area north of LA, called Hawthorne. After Della got too sick to handle me, I was off to the home of her friends and neighbors, Albert and Ida Bolender. This was the first real family-style home I lived in. I don't remember them too well but I do know they were good people. The Bolenders had a son named Lester, and they had a puppy named Tippy. Good ole Tippy. I was pretty happy as near as I can remember. At least, I mean, I don't recall being unhappy. But then a neighbor shot Tippy with a gun. I think that was the saddest I've ever been. I remember crying my eyes out. We buried Tippy in our backyard.

My mom was working at that time in the city for Columbia Pictures as a film cutter. She came to visit me and grandmother on weekends, most of the time anyway. She and grandma constantly argued about everything. Finally, when I was about 7 years old I went to live with my mom in a small house in Hollywood.

Even though it was mom's house, we shared it with another family, the Atkinsons from England. Mr. and Mrs. Atkinson were actors, the first actors I ever met. We were like one big happy family. Mom had a friend, a woman named Grace McKee who she met at work. She was mom's closest friend, and pretty soon she was my closest friend too. Anyway, things started happening, and pretty soon it was clear that mom wasn't well, and after she got laid off from Columbia, she suffered a nervous breakdown and she was hospitalized. I continued to live with Atkinsons, until they decided to move back to England. That's when Grace stepped in and cared for me like a foster-mother. God only knows where I would have ended up if it wasn't for Grace.

Grace quickly had herself appointed guardian over both mom and me. She sold the house, settled all our financial problems and moved me into her mother's house while she petitioned the court for my custody. But then Grace got married, and there wasn't a place for me in her small home with her husband Doc Goddard and his daughter by a previous marriage Nona, so Grace took me to the Los Angeles Children's Home, where I lived for about a year and a half. Living in an orphanage is terrible for a child, but I felt luckier than most of the others because Grace and her sister Enid visited me almost every weekend. We visited mom in the hospital a couple of times, and sometimes we went to lunch at the Ambassador Hotel and saw a movie afterwards. But it was obvious my mom was not normal. She was always very sad, withdrawn and kind of ... boring really. She was a good woman, Grace told me that, but she was very troubled. So Grace decided to keep me away from her for my own good.

Grace took me out often, and she bought me all kinds of nice clothes and shoes, and things. I remember one time, we went up on the roof of the orphanage together. She pointed out the water tower of RKO Pictures to me. "That's where I used to work," she said. "and one day, you're gonna work there too!"

Lights go back up. Jerry is at the piano, playing something soft.

Jerry:
Okay, so what happened after Grace got married? I remember she put you in the orphanage, but you said you didn't stay there very long. What happened after that?

Marilyn:
Oh, it was a mess. Grace did the best she could, and she did a lot for me it's true, but her new husband was a bastard. She was unhappy and she didn't want to expose me to him. So after a couple of months living with them, she asked my uncle Marion's wife to take me in. She was living in Compton with her mom and my three little cousins, Jack, Ida Mae and Olive.

Jerry:
Was he your mom's brother?

Marilyn:
Yes, her only brother; he was a few years younger than her. The only other relation I had was my grandma's sister in Portland, Aunt Dora.

Jerry:
What about your father? What ever happened to him?

Marilyn:
I never knew my father, and even then, I'm not sure if he really was my father. I don't even know if my mother was sure who my father was. It's very complicated and my mom never discussed it. Never. I do know this. Mortensen,

who was my mother's husband when she was pregnant with me, hadn't died before I was born. Another fellow with his exact name had been killed in a car crash in Ohio, and mom was told it was him who died. So he's still around, somewhere, maybe. But like I said, I'm not even sure he's my biological father. Nobody knows, I guess.

Jerry:
I see. So you went to live with your Uncle Marion and his wife and family.

Marilyn:
I never lived with my Uncle Marion, only with his wife Aunt Olive and her mother Auntie Ida Martin. You see, Marion disappeared back in 1929, when the children were just little kids. It was strange. He just went to the store one day to buy a newspaper and he was never seen again. Never.

Jerry:
Is that right? They never found him? Or they found him but, didn't tell you kids?

Marilyn:
No, no. They never found him, and his wife later had him presumed dead so she and the

family could collect welfare. Remember, this was during the Depression. Times were hard for everyone then. By the time I came to live with them in her mama's house, Uncle Marion hadn't been heard from for seven or eight years.

Jerry:
No kidding, that's sad!

Marilyn:
Very sad! Everyone in my family, from my grandparents, my mom and my uncle, all of them, had tragic lives. Even my half-brother Jackie died when he was just 14. My family's a real mess, Jerry, let me tell ya'.

Jerry:
Don't worry about it Norma Jean, my family's mostly still alive but they're a mess too!

Marilyn:
Is that supposed to make me feel better?

Jerry:
Yes.

They both laugh at themselves.

Did your mother know what happened to her baby brother? I mean that he disappeared without a trace?

Marilyn:

She knew. It was just another bit of crushing news to her. My mother was a sad person, and I suppose, when you think about it, she had every reason to be sad. No wonder she lost her mind, with all she had to endure. Poor sweet thing. She's still alive, you know.

Jerry:

Is she? I didn't know. Where is she today and what does she think about your success?

Marilyn:

She's in a nursing home in California. I don't think she realizes what's become of her daughter. She just tells me to save my money for a rainy day, and that kind of thing. I don't visit her anymore. She really doesn't care about anything. She's a Christian Scientist so she reads the Bible a lot. End of story.

Jerry:

That's a shame. Poor woman.

Marilyn starts weeping. Lights do down.

Act II

Two months later. Same scene, except now a dressing screen with sheer blinds is set up at stage left. Behind it is a dress rack and a table for accessories. Marilyn is sitting on the piano bench. She is lightly singing the song from Ladies of the Chorus "Every lady needs a dad, dad, daddy... ." Jerry enters from stage right, with a towel in his hands. He sits next to her and starts to play along as she sings. When they are finished they both laugh.

Jerry:
Hello, my dear. How have you been?

Marilyn:
Oh Jerry, you can't believe how much I've missed our little chats. I couldn't wait to get back to New York to see you. I want you to know, I've been giving our show a lot of thought. I have lots of ideas!

Jerry:
That's great, Marilyn, because I seem to have acquired a mental block.

Marilyn:
Would you like the name and number of a good therapist?

Jerry:

No thank you. (He pulls a bottle of whiskey from his pocket and takes a drink.) That's the only therapy I need! Would you care for a swig?

Marilyn:

I think I'll pass. Besides, I just had a breath mint.

Jerry:

Okay, let's see. Where were we?

Marilyn:

Jerry. (She slowly walks across the stage, thinking. He gazes upon her walk.) I have been giving our show a lot of thought. And frankly, I'm stumped. I don't want to make it too personal; God knows the public is bored with my private life.

Jerry:

It's up to you.

Marilyn:

(Continues thinking on her feet.) I want people to understand that Marilyn Monroe is a woman.

Jerry:

I doubt anybody needs convincing of that!

Marilyn:
Oh Jerry, you know what I mean. I'm not that one dimensional blonde bombshell I'm made out to be. I can play her well enough, but that's not really me. I want people to see the other side of me, the Norma Jean side too.

Jerry:
What are you talking about?

Marilyn:
I was reading about something. You know how in the old days kings and queens referred to themselves as "us" and "we?"

Jerry:
Yes, I think so.

Marilyn:
(She moves and sways and turns thoughtlessly.) Well that got me thinking. Sometimes I refer to Marilyn Monroe and myself as "us." You know, like we are two different people.

Jerry:
I'm not following you...

Marilyn:
You know...Norma Jean and Marilyn. Marilyn and Norma Jean.

Jerry:

I think you'll be confusing the issue. People are going to want to be entertained. If you throw a lot of spilt-personality stuff at them then it may get difficult.

Marilyn:

Jerry. You're my musical director not my analyst. And I'm not talking about spilt-personality stuff here, I'm talking about drama! You know there was a time when I was going to play Chekov. And right here in New York. I won two Golden Globes, you know, and several other acting awards.

Jerry:

I'm not opposed to a little drama.

Marilyn:

And I took considerable acting lessons. And dance lessons and I had vocal training. And I always studied with the best! So I want to put it all to good use.

Jerry:

Great. Let's get started.

Marilyn:

(Excitedly) What's our first number?

Jerry:
(He stares at her, admitting he has no idea how to answer her question.) I thought this was your show. You tell me what's the first number.

Marilyn:
Jerry! You're supposed to help me.

Jerry:
Let's work on it together. Now, where were we? Where were we?

Marilyn disappears behind the dressing screen. She starts to strip, and in so doing titillates Jerry and the audience.

Marilyn:
(From behind the screen.) We were talking about that boring stuff from my past.

Jerry:
I see you brought a change of clothes.

Marilyn:
(From behind the screen.) More than one!

Jerry:
Have you told anybody we're working together?

Marilyn:
Not a soul. (Marilyn reappears, dressed in the red dress from *Niagara*.). Look familiar?

Jerry:
Marilyn Monroe?

Marilyn:
Marilyn Monroe as Rose Loomis in *Niagara*. Did you see that one?

Jerry:
Sorry.

Marilyn:
Jerry, I'm surprised. It was one of my greatest performances.

Jerry:
Sorry.

Marilyn:
Well, you missed a good one. They even changed the name of Niagara Falls, New York to "Marilyn Monroe, New York" on the day of the premiere. We had a big parade and everything. That was a time when being Marilyn Monroe was still fun.

Jerry:
You mean it's not fun any more?

Marilyn:
(Thinking) Well, I don't want to sound ungrateful, but it is burdensome at times. You can't believe the demands made on my time. I get hundreds of invitations and appearance requests every week. It's horrible! And then there's the social obligations, the mail, the photographers, the reporters, the studio bosses, my agents, my lawyers, my doctors. And there's just little old me. Simple little Norma Jean Baker. It all got to me, let me tell ya'. There was a time I could barely face the new day. I had several physical problems; I was losing and then gaining weight like a yo-yo; emotionally I was a wreck. Even my hair was a mess. I went whole three weeks without brushing my hair. If you knew me before, you'd know that is unthinkable.

Jerry:
I imagine.

Marilyn:
Here I was, I thought, the biggest star in Hollywood, so they say. Great looks, great body, pretty smart for not having an education, great career, great future...and I was miserable. And

worst of all, I felt so guilty for being unhappy. What right did I have to be sad? I had everything you could ever desire. Everything. And I couldn't stop crying.

Imagine that?

Jerry:
You know what they say, be careful what you wish for, it may just come true. So tell me, how do you handle it all?

Marilyn:
It's not easy. But I'm past the breaking point, of this I'm sure. I've told everybody I'm temporarily retired. This way I can concentrate on our work together. This show is the most important thing to me now. I want to knock the people off their seats. I want to show them that Marilyn Monroe is more than just Marilyn Monroe. That I'm more than Marilyn Monroe. (She looks at herself in the imaginary mirror.)

Jerry:
Looks to me like you enjoy being Marilyn Monroe.

Marilyn:
I like playing her, not being her. Over the past two years I've come to see how Marilyn is like a

character that I've been playing. And this character is so strong, and so damn popular, that it swallowed me up completely. It's only now that I see the light again. I, Norma Jean Baker, have survived my odyssey as Marilyn Monroe. What a wild ride it's been.

Jerry:
Is this the distinction you want to bring to the stage. Norma Jean playing Marilyn Monroe?

Marilyn:
At first I thought that's what I wanted to do. But I'm stronger than that now. Since we first met I've had a change of heart. I wanted to bare my soul before. I wanted to show my pain. Now, I don't feel the same pain. I feel liberated. I'm perfectly comfortable with myself as both Marilyn and Norma Jean.

Jerry:
Is this a revelation to you now? An epiphany, as we say in the theater?

Marilyn:
Jerry, it's a major breakthrough! So let's get down to business. About that first number... (She disappears behind the dressing screen.)

I was thinking maybe something up tempo. To get folks in the mood.

Jerry:

Something like, *Diamonds Are A Girl's Best Friend?*

Marilyn:

(From behind the screen.) Uh huh. What do you think?

Jerry:

Let's do it. (He begins playing at the piano.)

Marilyn comes out in the famous dress from Gentlemen Prefer Blondes.

Marilyn:

(Sings and acts out "Diamonds")

Jerry:

Now we're talkin'. That's Marilyn Monroe! (He claps for her.)

Marilyn:

I did that song five times a day for three days in a row in Korea, when I was over there for the USO entertaining the troops. What a whirlwind that trip was.

Jerry:
I'll bet the boys loved it.

Marilyn:
I loved it! I never felt so wanted in my whole life. The one thing I'll always remember about that trip was how many cameras were snapping my picture at the same time. I think you could've made a movie out of all those film negatives. If you pieced them together. That's what my mom did for a living when I was born. She was a film cutter for Columbia. That's where she met Auntie Grace.

Jerry:
Tell me about your aunt Grace. She was a major influence on you, so I understand.

Marilyn:
Grace was the one who taught me how to wear make-up. And how to carry myself. I was the daughter she never had. She more than anyone encouraged me to take up modeling and acting. I guess she's the one I have to thank *or blame* for my success.

Jerry:
How so?

Marilyn:

Grace groomed me like my mother never would. She told me how pretty I was. She took me to the movies and told how I should be up there on the screen! She made me see myself up there. She was the one who encouraged me to become a photo model even when my husband was against it. She's the one who drove me to appointments, took me to the dentist, helped me with my hair and clothing, everything! She was my first manager too.

Jerry:

What happened to her?

Marilyn:

Poor dear. She died alone about ten years ago, just when things were beginning to go my way. You know, I don't think there's anything more sad than dying alone, with nobody there to close your eyes. Some say she committed suicide, but I don't believe it. I think her poor small body just gave out on her. And she was a Christian Scientist too. She wouldn't take any medicine or go to the hospital when she needed to. The press made it look bad. Like I abandoned her once I became famous. But that's not true. We drifted apart, like people always do. But she was happy for me, and she kept a scrapbook of me that I still have today. She wouldn't commit suicide, not Grace. I once read that suicide is worse than murder because in a murder you only kill one or two people. But with a suicide you kill the whole world. Grace would never do that! (Pauses.) But let's not get all teary-eyed. We've got a show to produce.

She darts off behind the dressing screen.

Jerry:
(To audience.) It was then that I realized the two aspects of her character, not the Norma Jean slash Marilyn aspects she cares about, but the alternately sad and euphoric parts of her personality. I didn't want to call anybody to find out more about her because we're supposed to be working in private, and I respect that's the way she wants it. She's obviously suffered a great deal of loss and loneliness; three broken marriages, fights with the studio over the direction of her career. I can empathize with her struggles, who couldn't? And I did do some reading up on her in books and magazines. I also, very slyly I might add, spoke to a few people who've worked with her in the past. I came away from these chats with a kind of confirmation of my

own thoughts and conclusions about her (He stands up and walks upstage as he explains.) I don't think she is nearly as insecure as most people make her out to be. Her problem is she's convinced she has gotten where she is on looks alone and not on talent. She may be right of course, but that doesn't mean she doesn't have talent. I think she's proven herself in musicals and comedies, and some of her dramatic roles were well received too. Of course, the critics are hard on her as a general rule but she does have her champions. I think I'm slowly becoming one myself.

Marilyn:

(From behind dressing screen.) Jerry! Have you seen my pink panties?

Light go down. End of Act II.

Act III

Jerry is sitting at the table flipping through magazines. He glances at his watch and then at the door. He is impatient. Finally, after a moment, he grabs his hat and coat and prepares to leave. He turns out the lights and opens the door to leave. Marilyn is there, having just arrived.

Marilyn:

Oh Jerry, sorry I'm late. Please forgive me. My day has been murder. Fox is trying to get me to star in another hair-brained musical. They're making my life more than miserable. I hate them!

Jerry:

You're two hours late! You could have called.

Marilyn:

You never gave me the phone number.

Jerry:

No? All right, come on in. We can get a little work in anyway.

Marilyn:

I'm sorry Jer... Don't be mad at me, please.

Jerry:

I'm not mad at you. I'm mad at myself. For the entire time I waited for you I didn't come up with a single idea. Frankly Marilyn, I'm not sure I'm the right guy for you.

Marilyn:

Jerry, what are you talking about? I've seen your work. You're top notch. You're perfect for me. Besides, we like each other. Don't we..?

Jerry:

That's not the point. I frequently work with folks I can't stand. In fact, the worst folks usually pay the best.

Marilyn:

Jerry, that reminds me. We've never talked about how much I'm supposed to be paying you. I hope I can afford you.

Jerry:

Until I can get something down on paper, I haven't earned anything yet.

Marilyn:

Well, you let me know and I'll have my manager write you a check. I don't handle money any more. I find that if I have $20 in my purse I spend it immediately. If I don't carry any money, I never think of spending it.

Jerry:
Okay, well let's get going.

Marilyn:
(She gets comfortable.) So, what's our second number?

Jerry:
Don't you think we need some dialogue between numbers?

Marilyn:
You know, it's a funny thing. I was thinking the same thing. Do you know anybody who can write it for us?

Jerry:
Why don't you write it yourself.

Marilyn:
Oh heavens, no. I couldn't do that. I'm not a writer.

Jerry:
Sure you can. You don't have to be a writer. You've got something no other writer's got.

Marilyn:
What's that?

Jerry:
You've got the inside story. You have your own feelings. It's your story, after all. Only you can write it honestly.

Marilyn:
Well, I don't know. I'd be willing to help out. But I'd need a collaborator, just like you.

Jerry:
You've got your collaborator. Norma Jean Baker, remember?

Marilyn:
Yeah, you're right. You're right. (Thinking on her feet.) I have written a little bit of poetry. And I write letters all the time. (Pause.) You know, this could be good. Very good. But it's got to be entertaining. You know how I feel about personal stuff. But if we keep it light and frothy...

Jerry:
...Very frothy.

Marilyn:
...We can show 'em all. Let's see. I'll where my blue chiffon dress, shoulderless of course, and a smart hat from this groovy little shop on

57th Street. I can see it now, footlights around the stage, opening night. In the audience are all my friends, and big stars like Betty Grable, Rita Hayworth, and, and Frank Sinatra. They, of course, will have no idea what I'm about to do. But I'll knock 'em dead. Every one of them! And the critics will all have heart attacks because they won't be able to knock me. (Laughing) It's going to be wonderful Jerry, and all because of you.

Jerry:
Whoa, whoa, whoa. I haven't even started yet. We've got a long way to go to opening night.

Marilyn:
I just had an idea. Let's do it one night only. This way, if you didn't see it you've missed it forever.

Jerry:
Marilyn, the whole idea of the theater is to perform on the stage night after night.

Marilyn:
Jerry, you know I don't have time for that. I've got two movies scheduled. That'll take me to the middle of next year. We can plan this for next Fall. How does that sound?

Jerry:
I'm not sure I want to get involved if you only want to do one performance. I can't see it.

Marilyn:
Wait, I just had another idea. What do you say we film it? I have my own production company, you know. We can film it and release it as a movie with Fox. I still owe them a movie and maybe they'll take this one. We'd be killing two birds with one stone. (Still twirling and thinking aloud.) Yes, I can see it very clearly. A whole new kind of movie.

Jerry:
Kind of like a documentary that's not a real documentary?.

Marilyn:
Yeah. Like a performance movie or something. I like that. I think the studio will too. And it'll be tons cheaper than making a traditional film. See, we're making progress. (Excitedly) So, tell me, what's our second number?

Jerry:
Marilyn, ya' gotta give the audience what they expect. This is a fundamental rule of the stage. What do you think everyone will want to hear?

Marilyn:

(Dashing off behind the dressing screen.) Um, *I Wanna Be Loved By You?*

Jerry:

Well, that's what all the men will want.

Marilyn:

How about if I go down into the audience and choose a man, and sing it to him?

Jerry:

That's an idea. (To himself) The lucky bugger...

Marilyn:

(Still behind the dressing screen.) Do you know how to play it?

Jerry:

I think I can figure it out. (He plays the introductory notes to the song.)

Marilyn appears in the blue dress she described earlier. She's prances sexily toward Jerry.

Marilyn:

I'll pretend you're the man.

Jerry:

I'll pretend too.

Marilyn:

(She sings the song and playfully acts it out.)

That was wonderful! I haven't sang that song since...since...well, never mind.

Jerry:

You're not trying to hide something from me?

Marilyn:

Jerry, how could I hide a thing from you? How can I hide a single thing from anybody? It seems the whole world knows everything about me. It's horrible. I sometimes find myself fantasizing that I'm a woman of mystery and disguise. You know, I love walking around New York with a dark wig and sun glasses, in a frumpy coat. Nobody ever recognizes me. It's so refreshing, and reaffirming. You know, sometimes I have to get outside and walk around just to convince myself I'm still alive and free. You can't believe how my handlers try to protect me. They're afraid I'm going to get kidnapped, or that I'm going to trip over some bump somewhere and bruise myself something awful. But I steel away into the night to fight the isolation. That's why I like living in New York. In LA, you can go out after midnight and everything is closed. But not New York. It's like the wild west in the east! Anyway, I love torturing them; see how it feels. (Laughing) Am I terrible?

Jerry:
Naw, I suppose that's natural enough. But I've always believed life is just the sum of our own choices. You have to make your own decisions. Otherwise you'll wake up one day full of regret and remorse.

Marilyn:
That's good Jerry. I like that. Maybe we can work that sentiment into the play somewhere. Let me write it down. (She searches for a pen. He has a pencil behind his ear and hands it to her.) Jerry, what was that one again? Say it to me slowly so I can get it right.

Jerry:
I just said that life is the sum total of the decisions we make for ourselves. If we are unhappy, than we've made the wrong decisions, since happiness is, presumably, our greatest purpose on earth.

Marilyn:
(Writing and repeating.) "Happiness is our greatest purpose on earth." I like that. I think peoples' happiness is too often neglected. It's

either overlooked or taken for granted. But it's something I work on for myself all the time?

Jerry:

How's it going?

Marilyn:

That's a good question. I struggle with my happiness. I know I have a lot going for myself, but I'm afraid of losing it. Not just of losing it, no. I'm afraid of squandering it; of letting it fall through my hands, so to speak. So I've been training myself to be vigilant; that's not my word, that's my doctor's word. I feel I need to be prepared to face the future with understanding, and with confidence. This seems to be my idea of happiness. You have to fight for it or risk losing it.

Jerry:

Sounds pretty brutal.

Marilyn:

It is. I remember this one reporter asked me if I was happy when I won the Golden Globe for *Some Lie It Hot*. But he added the word, "now" at the end of his question. He asked, "Are you happy now?" like maybe I wasn't before. That got me thinking. Is there this perception that I'm unhappy? And if so, what a terrible thing to do to the people. (She get up and walks around.) Sometimes, when I'm alone, which is how I prefer to be nowadays, time seems to standstill, especially in the middle of the night. That's when I do my thinking. (Pause) I've learned that the things that are important to me don't change, it's we who change. The important things stay the same. I call them the Permanent Things. (Pause) I'm not talking about good health or happiness or anything like that. I'm talking about goodness. There's so much goodness in the world, and we have to keep reminding ourselves to see it and feel it.

Jerry:
And recognize it when we see it and feel it?

Marilyn:
Exactly. You know, Jerry. I find these little chats of ours very uplifting. I think maybe it proves that I need someone to talk to. And you know, that person doesn't have to be a doctor or a Ph D.

Jerry:
Bingo. Another revelation!

Marilyn:

(To herself.) Yeah. (To Jerry.) What do ya' say we work on another number? But let's do something different this time. How about we do something for the ladies in the audience?

Jerry:

Marilyn, are you sure you want to do a play? I mean, the stage is lot different from a movie set. There are no re-takes in live theater.

Marilyn:

I know, Jerry. That's exactly why I want to do it. Why I have to do it. I want to prove to myself that I *can* do it. You know I almost played Gushinka once.

Jerry:

Are you doing this for yourself or to prove something to others?

Marilyn:

Jerry, I've learned not to concern myself about what others think. I use to let it bother me something awful. I couldn't sleep sometimes if someone said something hurtful, or if a critic panned me. I had to take sleeping pills or I would toss and turn all night. Even when I was married. Then in the mornings, especially if we were shooting, I'd have to take pep pills to shake off the affect of the sleeping pills. It was a crazy cycle. Then I just decided to save myself. Forget about what others think. It was destroying me. Now I care about what I think most of all. (Pauses as she continues to think.) Does that sound selfish?

Jerry:

I suppose it does in a way, but you're no ordinary woman. You're Marilyn Monroe; Norma Jean, whatever. You're a special case.

Marilyn:

Do you really think so?

Jerry:

Sure I do. Its not easy being famous, I know that. It's just that the average person doesn't think in those terms when they see you. So my advice is to be the way you want in private, but in public don't let it show.

Marilyn:

You're right. You know I've always been one of those who wears her heart on her sleeve. What you're saying, is if I'm vulnerable, don't let it show because it only makes me feel that way more.

Jerry:

I suppose what I'm saying is don't be so vulnerable in the first place.

Marilyn:

I see.

Jerry:

If you want to prove something to yourself, you should consider doing it in private first. I think the public theater is not the place for that sort of thing. You might be accused of self-indulgence. Even if you do it only one time.

Marilyn:

But that's where good writing comes in. You know, I'm glad we had this conversation. It's getting late and I've held you long enough. (She looks at her watch.) Yes, it's very late and my driver is waiting outside. He's probably sleeping by now. What do you say we pick it backup next week? Tuesday maybe?

Jerry:

I'm going away this weekend. I won't be back for three weeks.

Marilyn:

No? Well, we'll have to work out our schedules. Can I have my secretary call you?

Jerry:
Sure, in three weeks.

Marilyn:
And think about those numbers, especially the one for the ladies. (She picks up her hat and coat.) We can't forget the ladies!

Jerry:
Of course not. Good night Marilyn. (She approaches him and kisses him on the cheek.)

Marilyn:
Good night Jerry. Have good trip. And give my regards to Mrs. Ross.

Jerry:
I will. Take care of yourself. And promise me you won't think so much.

He rises to escort her out the door, and as he opens it, she curtsies.

Marilyn:
Funny, you're not the first one to tell me that. Okay, good night. And get some sleep. See you soon.

She kisses him once more and exits.

Jerry:

Jerry rubs the back of his neck, stretches his back and then lightly touches his cheek. He looks at his hand as if to see evidence of the kisses. He pours himself a drink and returns to the piano.

(He sings *Growing New You*.):

> Light the candle by your bed, lay down your head
> No book, no music, no dreaming, just lie there like you're dead
> Hear a cat call in the street, see the stars at their peak.
> Everyone knows where they're goin' but to you it seems so empty
> Yes, I know what you're going through
> You're a prisoner of doubt on the inside looking out
> And you haven't got a clue. Oh
> All of the suffering you do there's a growing new you.
> You don't talk about success cuz you don't think like all the rest do
> You tell yourself its all making sense somewhere
> and there will come a rescue
> And you try and do your best, so you buy a brand new dress

You force yourself to go to their parties
but it all seems so grotesque.
Yea, I know that life can be cruel
First you hurt till you cry then you cry till
you laugh
Is this what you deserve. No.
All of the suffering you do, there's a
growing new you.
Yes, I know what you're going through
But you need all the pain, like a flower
needs the rain
It's real and it's true, so
All of the suffering you do
All of the suffering you do
All you ever do is growing new you.*

He continues to play the piano. He then returns to the audience as he plays and wistfully says:

That was the last time I saw Marilyn. Norma Jean. Whoever. About four months later I got a check in the mail. No letter, just a check. I guess she changed her mind about doing the show. (He repeats last refrain of the song. Marilyn appears on the stage, looking down, then dramatically upwards as he concludes.)

Lights go down slowly over him and a moment later over her.

Finis

*Words & Music by Dirk Hamilton, copyright 1979 Rabbit Songs, BMI. Used by permission.

About the Author

Author of *Who Said That?* and more than a dozen books and plays, J. Ajlouny holds a B.A. in Journalism from Wayne State University and a J.D. from Michigan State University. He founded the Federal Bureau of Entertainment (FBE) to develop and produce one-person stage shows featuring prominent British actors. Now focusing on touring theatre projects and Great Lakes history research, he is a writer and editor of humor, pop-reference, essays, and assorted arcana. He lives in Detroit.

Fresh Ink Group

Publishing
Free Memberships
Share & Read Free Stories, Essays, Articles
Free-Story Newsletter
Writing Contests

🖉

Books
E-books
Amazon Bookstore

🖉

Authors
Editors
Artists
Professionals
Publishing Services
Publisher Resources

🖉

Members' Websites
Members' Blogs
Social Media

Email: info@FreshInkGroup.com
Twitter: @FreshInkGroup
Google+: Fresh Ink Group
Facebook.com/FreshInkGroup
LinkedIn: Fresh Ink Group
About.me/FreshInkGroup

Fresh Ink Group
Guntersville

Meet William Shakespeare

Much has been explored about Shakespeare and his life, but little is known about how this small-town boy with a grammar-school education came to pen masterworks like *Hamlet* and *King Lear*. In *Meet William Shakespeare*, playwright J. Ajlouny creates authentic and plausible explanations that answer centuries-old questions about the man and his work. The result is an educational and fun portrait of Shakespeare, as told by The Bard himself.

Push Pull Press/Fresh Ink Group

THE TRIAL OF WILLIAM SHAKESPEARE

Few men have endured the indignity of having their very existence challenged as thoroughly as William Shakespeare, late of Stratford-upon-Avon. From scholars to amateur enthusiasts, many cannot bring themselves to believe he wrote his own body of work. Playwright J. Ajlouny presents the arguments for and against, all statements and proofs drawn from the historical record. Everybody must decide for himself, but *The Trial of William Shakespeare* makes the controversy both intriguing and fun.

Push Pull Press/Fresh Ink Group

WHO SAID THAT?

Who Said That? provides an entertaining and authoritative reference for the origins and meanings of our common figures of speech.

- Who said 100+ famous expressions?
- Who *really* said them?
- What did they actually say?
- What did they actually mean?
- Why did they say them that way?
- Who repeated what was said?

Surprisingly true, sometimes strange, always fascinating, the stories about whence came these expressions will entertain, educate, and even amaze you.

Push Pull Press/Fresh Ink Group

FIGURATIVELY SPEAKING

A "Figure of speech" is an expression that creates a more forceful or dramatic meaning, such as "stretch the truth" or "baptism by fire." We finally have a thesaurus to discover their origins and the sources of their meanings. Whether reading it for fun, researching phrases you use, or studying the symbolic foundations of our language, Figuratively Speaking is the resource you'll reach for time and again.

Push Pull Press/Fresh Ink Group

www.ingramcontent.com/pod-product-compliance
Lightning Source LLC
Chambersburg PA
CBHW071415040426
42444CB00009B/2257